Ticks

Ticks

Patrick Merrick

THE CHILD'S WORLD®, INC.

Library of Congress Cataloging-in-Publication Data
Merrick, Patrick.
Ticks/Patrick Merrick.
p. cm.
Includes index.
Summary: Introduces the physical characteristics,
behavior, and life cycle of ticks.
ISBN 1-56766-384-2 (lib. bdg.:alk. paper)
1. Ticks—Juvenile literature. [1. ticks.] I. Title.
QL458.M53 1997
595.4'29—dc21 96-47082
CIP
AC

Photo Credits

COVER CREDIT HERE:
Robert & Linda Mitchell: cover, 2, 10, 15, 20, 26, 30
COMSTOCK/Jack K. Clark: 6, 9, 13, 16
COMSTOCK/Russ Kinne, 19
Joe McDonald: 23
Leonard Lee Rue/Tony Stone Images, 24
Robert Brons/BPS/Tony Stone Images: 29

On the cover...

Front cover: This tick is balanced on a leaf.
Page 2: Soft ticks like this one have a soft body.

Table of Contents

When the weather gets warmer, people like to spend lots of time outside. They like to hike through tall grass and go exploring in the woods. Being outside is lots of fun! But we need to be careful. Some of the creatures that live outside can make us itch or even make us sick. One of these creatures is the tick.

This tick is walking on a person's hand.

What Do Ticks Look Like?

Ticks look a lot like other summertime bugs, but they are quite different. Most bugs are insects. But ticks belong to another animal family called **arachnids**. Mites, scorpions, and spiders are arachnids, too. Arachnids have eight legs. They also have bodies with two parts. One part contains the head and chest. The other part is the **abdomen**, which contains the stomach.

All ticks have a small head and a large abdomen.

How Many Kinds of Ticks Are There?

There are about 800 different kinds, or **species**, of ticks in the world. Most ticks are either gray or brown. Some are as small as a tiny little dot. Others are an inch long! Scientists divide these tick species into two groups. *Hard-body ticks* are flatter and have a hard shell protecting most of their body. *Soft-body ticks* are rounder and don't have a full shell.

Soft-body ticks like this one don't have full shells to protect them.

What Do Ticks Eat?

Ticks eat only one thing—blood! They are **parasites**, which means that they live and feed on other animals. Ticks suck blood from birds, reptiles, and even people.

Ticks find an animal by sensing its breath. If the tick is close enough, it simply grabs onto the animal's fur, feathers, or skin. These tiny parasites can also crawl. They might crawl as far as 15 feet to get to an animal. But they cannot fly or jump.

This *Pajaheullo tick* is feeding on a cow.

How Do Ticks Eat?

A tick has a mouth shaped like a hook. This hook keeps the tick from falling off the animal while it is feeding. First the tick bites the animal and makes a small hole. Then it sticks the hook inside the hole. Once the hook is under the animal's skin, the tick starts sucking blood. The tick stays attached to the animal and feeds until it is full.

A tick's body is designed to hold lots of blood. Its stomach has folds of skin that can grow as the tick feeds. The tick can grow to 25 or 30 times its normal size. If you could do this, you would grow to 90 feet tall just by eating a big dinner!

If you look closely, you can see the tick's hook under this person's skin.

Adult ticks mate after they feed on an animal. Once they have mated, most of the male ticks die. The female ticks quickly lay up to 18,000 eggs. They lay their eggs in plants or inside dead leaves. After laying the eggs, the females also die.

Sometimes the eggs take up to six months to hatch. Once the eggs hatch, the baby ticks are called **larvae**. These tick larvae are also called "seed ticks" because they look like little seeds. The tiny seed ticks crawl into the grass and attach themselves to passing animals. Once they are attached, the larvae feed on the animals.

Female ticks like this one can lay thousands of eggs at one time.

What Is a Tick's Skin Like?

Seed ticks grow larger as they eat. But because of their shell-like skin, they grow differently from people. When a seed tick gets too big for its skin, it stops feeding and drops off the animal. Then it wriggles out of its old, outgrown skin! This is called **molting**. The tick has a new and bigger skin underneath. After the tick molts, it finds a new animal and starts feeding again. Seed ticks go through these steps of feeding and molting three to seven times. After the seed tick molts for the last time, it finally becomes an adult.

This tick's skin is stretched from feeding.

Ticks live wherever they can find animals to feed on. They live in every state of the United States and almost every country in the world. Ticks love places with lots of tall grass, weeds, bushes, and piles of dead grass and leaves. They normally live outdoors. Sometimes, though, they fasten themselves to people or pets. Then they can end up in people's yards or homes.

These soft body ticks are crawling in the wet dirt.

Do Any Animals Eat Ticks?

With their tough skins and small bodies, ticks don't have a lot of enemies. However, some birds love to eat ticks! The best known of these birds is called the *tickbird*. Tickbirds ride around on giraffes, buffaloes, rhinos, and other large animals. They pick the ticks off the animal's skin. This helps the animal and makes a nice meal for the tickbird, too.

This tickbird, called an *oxpecker*, is riding on a water buffalo.

Most tick bites don't cause major problems. But some ticks can make people and other animals very sick. Some ticks carry illnesses, such as Rocky Mountain spotted fever and Lyme disease. These illnesses can be dangerous, so it is important to learn how to protect yourself from ticks.

If you are going to a place that might have ticks, wear long pants and a long-sleeved shirt. It's easier to spot ticks if your clothes are light-colored. Tucking your pants into your socks or boots makes it hard for ticks to reach your skin. It's also a good idea to put bug spray on your clothes to make the ticks stay away.

This *American dog tick* is sucking blood from a person's arm.

Check your clothes, skin, and hair for ticks while you are still outside. That way they can't come into your house with you! Check your pets, too, to make sure they don't have any ticks riding along.

This soft-body tick is waiting on a rock for its next meal.

If you do find a tick on you, stay calm. Remember, most ticks don't carry diseases. And maybe the tick hasn't even attached itself yet. It might still be crawling around. Look closely at it. Does it already have its hook underneath your skin? You'll need to use tweezers to gently pull the tick out. Your mom or dad can help you do this. After you remove the tick, put it in alcohol or boiling water to kill it. Don't throw the tick in the garbage or back outside because it might attach itself to someone else.

This tick is attached to a person's skin.

Many people are scared of ticks because they think tick bites will hurt them. Other people find ticks scary because they suck blood. The truth is, ticks suck blood for the same reason you eat a sandwich—because it is good for them and it helps them grow. Ticks might seem like pests, but they are also a normal part of the natural world. If we are careful, we can enjoy the outdoors without worrying about the tick.

This soft-body tick is sitting on a rock.

Glossary

abdomen (AB–duh–men)
The abdomen is the stomach area of a tick.

arachnids (uh-RAK-nid)
Arachnids are animals that have eight legs and a body divided into two parts. Ticks, spiders, and scorpions are arachnids.

larvae (LAR–vee)
Larvae are baby ticks. They are also called "seed ticks."

molting (MOLT)
Molting is getting rid of an old, outgrown skin. Baby ticks molt several times as they grow.

parasite (PARE-uh-site)
A parasite is an animal that lives and feeds on other animals. Ticks are parasites.

species (SPEE-sheez)
A species is a different kind of an animal. There are about 800 species of ticks.

Index